PEN AND PAPER

PEN AND PAPER

CHARRON MOLLETTE

PEN AND PAPER

iUniverse books may be ordered through booksellers or by contacting:

iUniverse
1663 Liberty Drive
Bloomington, IN 47403
www.iuniverse.com
1-800-Authors (1-800-288-4677)

Because of the dynamic nature of the Internet, any web addresses or links contained in this book may have changed since publication and may no longer be valid. The views expressed in this work are solely those of the author and do not necessarily reflect the views of the publisher, and the publisher hereby disclaims any responsibility for them.

Any people depicted in stock imagery provided by Thinkstock are models, and such images are being used for illustrative purposes only. Certain stock imagery © Thinkstock.

ISBN: 978-1-5320-0882-5 (sc)
ISBN: 978-1-5320-0883-2 (e)

Library of Congress Control Number: 2016917039

Print information available on the last page.

iUniverse rev. date: 10/06/2016

CONTENTS

This book is dedicated to my daughter Jerrelle Ann

ACKNOWLEDGEMENTS

To my mom and dad, Ann R. DeWitty and Clifford R. Mollette, for always being there and supporting me. To my teacher, Sister Mary Annette at Holy Names Academy, for always encouraging me to keep on writing. And to all the other poets and hip hop artists of the world. And last but not least, to my soulmate Lucky, for his inspiration and dedicated enthusiasm during this project.

Charron Marie Mollette currently resides in Kent, WA. Her previous work was included in the book "Under the Harvest Moon" where she received the Editors Choice Award' from the National Library of Poetry.

A huge fan of authors Shel Silverstein and Robert Frost, she also enjoys Art Museums and playing bingo.

"Elvis"

He's the King of Rock & Roll, a "Kat" who can Swing...
He's Better than Brilliant, 'cause that's his Thing.
From Tupelo, Mississippi to Memphis, Tennessee...
It's Peanut Butter & Banana Sandwiches,
singing "That's All Right" with me.

He's a "Teddy Bear", with Black Hair, making Hollywood News...
by serenading a "Hound Dog", in his "Blue Suede Shoes".
A Pink Cadillac, at the Graceland Mansion,
the Home of his Guitar...
this Leading Man is Unforgettable, as a Singer & Movie Star.

"Don't be Cruel", Don't be Jealous, 'cause Fans follow his Flow...
"Girls, Girls, Girls" are "All Shook Up".
He's even Cooler than Snow.

This "King Creole", is full of Soul, dancing
to the "Jail House Rock"...
Capturing the Hearts of Teenagers, who wear Bobby-Socks.

He made "Heartbreak Hotel" Reservations,
in the Blue Hawaiian Sun...
Having "Fun in Acapulco", Clam-baking with Everyone.

He tells those with "Suspicious Minds", please "Treat Me Nice"…
Performing on the Las Vegas Stage, in a
Jumpsuit with Diamond Ice.

Since his appearance on Ed Sullivan, people will never forget…
this Legendary Entertainer, who did a Frank Sinatra Duet.

He's the King of Rock & Roll, a "Kat" who can Swing…
He's Better than Brilliant, 'cause that's his Thing.

Written By: Charron M. Mollette(*09)

"HORSE SHOE"

It's a Symbol of Good Luck, or Pegasus on a Quest…
It's the Sheriff & his Posse, chasin' Bandits out West.

It's Bear Tracks that are left, by a '65 Mustang…
with "Va-room Technology", givin' it more "Bang!"

It's "National Velvet" on the Silver Screen…
It's "The Ford Pinto", which is also a Bean.

It's the Mighty "Clydesdale" & "Budweiser" Beer…
It's "Palominos" Puddle-Jumping, showing no fear.

On the Racetrack, "Sea Biscuit", becomes a Hero…
His competition? Feeling Less than Zero.

It's Dale Evans & "Buttermilk", Roy Rogers & "Trigger"…
Larger than Life, their Hearts even Bigger.

It's the Jingle-Jangle, of Spurs, feelin' just Fine…
It's the "Justin Boot", a Square-Dancing "Hoot", since 1879.

It's Arabian Knights, through your Dreams, they Creep…
Your Pillows tell stories, while your fast asleep.

It's the Ride of Paul Revere, a Moment in History …
It's the Legend of Sleepy Hollow, which remains a Mystery.

It's the Heart of Horses, the Trailblazers of Flight…
Whose Free Spirit shall be, eternally Bright.

Written By: Charron M. Mollette (*16)

Sand Castle"

She's the Sway in Palm Trees, packed with Hawaiian Punch…
She Giggles because, She's Loved a Whole Bunch.

She's Sweeter than Sugar Cane. She's Pineapples on Pizza.
She's Seashells & Coral. A version of Mona Lisa.

She's a Tropical Breeze, of a Golden Sunrise…
She's that "Aloha" greeting, with Stars in her eyes.

She's more Fun, than a Hula Skirt needing a Barber…
She's from a place that honors, the Fallen Heroes of Pearl Harbor.

She's the Beauty of a Lai, a Necklace made of Flowers…
Some Snorkel or Scuba, but she plays with Dolphins for Hours.

Pardon me, while I Preach, about how she spreads Joy…
She's an Authentic Angel. A Pleasure as Poi.

She's that Impressive Sand Castle, on the Beach by the Sea…
She's a Bird of Paradise, She's Waikiki.

You'll go Coconuts, for her Cheery Smile…
You'll go Bananas, &Hug her for a while.

She's the Sway in Palm Trees, packed with Hawaiian Punch…
She Giggles because, She's Loved a Whole Bunch.

Written By: Charron M. Mollette (*07)

"Hot Comb"

She's the Hottest in Hair Sculpture, her Salon a second home…
Those wanting Glamour, get the Whip of her Comb.

There's no one quite like her, competition she Crushes…
A Conditioning Magician, with her Gift and Brushes.

"The Bob" roared in the Twenties. Scissors Clickity-Clack…
Angela Davis & the Afro, made it Cool to be Black.

She's Spunky & Funky, when she Finger waves…
A Quick Curling Wizard, unruly Hair behaves.

Bo Derek's Braids, scored a Perfect Ten…
She's a French-twisting Visionary, where everyone wins.

Pippy Long stocking's Ponytails, from Storybook Land…
can't beat her creations, made with Rubber bands.

A Hair Drying Icon, as Vidal Sasson…
Rumored she worked in Hollywood, when Cher struck the Moon.

She's Fairytale's Rapunzel, with Delightfully Dancing Curls...
She's more fearless than the Blonde Angel, one of Charlie's Girls.

She's Tony Award winning. She's the Toast of Broadway...
Hair, the musical, has been replaced, by this one woman play.

She's the Hottest in Hair Sculpture, her Salon a second home...
Those wanting Glamour, get the Whip of her Comb.

Written By: Charron M. Mollette (*13)

"Irish Rose"

"It's a Long way to Tipperary", as the melody goes...
The Well of Ara, running through it, as the Irish Rose.

Cows standing proudly, for their Butter-making skills...
The Maid of Erin and Martyr statues, garnishing the hamlet's hills.

Munster Rugby star, the infamous Alan Quinlan...
A native son of the quaint isle, his vision was to win.

A feisty red-head fell in love, with a Quiet Man named Sean...
At rainbow's end, her Golden dowry, guarded from Leprechauns.

Pastures of Four-Leaf Clovers, true believers granted Luck...
Misty rain is perfect weather, a "Happy Out" for any duck.

Two pints of gat, are on tap, at the corner Pub...
On St. Patrick's Day, "a Whale of a time",
in a Guinness filled bathtub.

"Doing the washing", some heirloom sweaters, are kept stain free…
While grabbing some biscuits from the press, as one "wets the Tea".

The Irish Setter, Best in Show, awarded Blue Ribbon loot…
A Good natured, bird-hunter, with mahogany fur boots.

Ireland's flag flew, Brigadier Meagher set the scene…
The White representing a truce, between the Orange and Green.
"It's a Long way to Tipperary", as the melody goes…
The Well of Ara, running through it, as the Irish Rose.

Written By: Charron M. Mollette (*16)

"Gone Fishing"

The Friendly Outdoorsman, to Owls & Woodchucks...
A "Gone Fishing" Bumper Sticker, on his Pick-Up Truck.

With a Wooden Tackle Box, he patiently awaits...
Catching Rainbow Trout, Night Crawlers for Bait.

A "Mosquito Bounty Hunter", armed
with Flashlights & Batteries...
Sleeping Bags, Roughing It, beneath Evergreen Trees.

Trail Mix It or Not, A Must Have? "Gooey" S'Mores...
Beef Jerky & Bottled Water, in Packs of Twenty-Four.

A True Leader. A True Heart. A True Eagle Scout...
The Jealous have been Jinxed, & Time is running out.

Black Bear or Cougars, he Out Wits & Out Stares...
Even Sly King Salmon, had better beware.

Around a small Campfire, his Ghost Stories tell why...
The Moon starts to Howl, as Stars fill the Night Sky.

As for the Myth "Sasquatch" or "Big Foot" to Most...
Some say, that he tamed it to eat Tuna on Toast.

No Doubt, he's the Truth, No Doubt, he's the Best...
He's no Sardine Fisherman, but a Legend on a Quest.

The Friendly Outdoorsman, to Owls& Woodchucks...
A "Gone Fishing" Bumper Sticker, on his Pick-Up Truck.

Written By; Charron M. Mollette (*08)

"MOMS ARE..."

More Awesome than Autumn or April Afternoons...
Spreading Happiness everywhere, as Bouquets of Balloons.

They're Cool as Iced Coffee. Critics. A Smash!
seen Cruising the Caribbean, while Calculating their Cash.

They're Hip as Downtown Dwellings, with Denim-colored Dens...
They Devote Decembers, signing Autographs in Pen.

They're Sweet as Embroidery, or Elm Trees at Birth...
Their Warm Hearts, cause Eclipses upon Mother Earth.

They're Fundamentally Fussy, about their Financial Funds...
They're Fallen Angels. Gifted Ones.

It's no Gimmick, they're Gracious, as Everyone knows...
They're Gems. They Glisten. They Glow.

How do they Heighten Harmony, with Effortless Force?
with Hilarious Humor, & Smiles of Course.

Their Internal Intuition, is hard to Ignore...
They're Hugs are Cozy as Igloos, they're not Idle Bores.

Just as Planet Jupiter, or the Beauty of Jade...
They're Unique, Triple Neat, as Jackets of Suede.

They're the Keepers of Kindness. Sheer Delights...
And Braver than a Ka-Zillion Medieval Knights.

They May have Lunch with the Ladies, by the Lakeside…
They're Good Listeners. Lionesses, who've got Pride.

Loving Mothers are Magicians, & a Mysterious Matrix…
They deal with Mild Mayhem. They're a Mozart Re-Mix.

They're Swell, in a Nutshell, No one can Compete…
From the Tip of their Nose, right down to their Feet.

They Overcomes Odd Obstacles, pressing Onward, like Oceans…
They have Outstanding Outlooks, in their Outreach Devotions.

They're Peachy. Philosophers. Sweeter than Pumpkin Pie…
They have Prizewinning Prose, & not afraid to Cry.

They're often Quoted, when Answering Questions…
Some fix Quiche Lorraine, as a Quick, Dinner Suggestion.

Here's a Little Reminder, it was Requested I mention…
That their Rimless Shades, cause "Hater Conventions".

The Sharpest Scholars of Science, & the Scribbles of Shakespeare…
They're Smooth as Sinatra, Singing "My Way" in your ears…

Un-cut & Unselfish, No words can Express…
They're the Very Utmost, in Urban City Finesse.

They're World Class Wonders, Quaint as a Xylophone
Cool as a Cucumber, or a Frozen Yogurt Cone.

With a "Zap!" & a "Zing!", Quicker than a Zip-Lock…
Their Smile is worth Zillions, Sparkling like Diamond Rocks.

Written By: Charron M. Mollette (*12)

~ 13 ~

"BANANA SPLIT"

Do you want to go Bananas, with a Savory Treat?
Or Frozen in Time, by the Ultimate Sweet?

More Flavor than Fiction, in a Crystal Dish…
It's what Cravings are made of. It's what Cookies wish.

Funny & Fresh Sliced Bananas, with no where to hide…
A Tropical Native. A Nutritious Inside.

Scoops of Pistachio, even Mint Chip will do…
Vanilla & Chocolate, Fresh Strawberries too.

You'll Utter & Stutter, over Butter Pecan…
On one Rocky Road, to a "Taste Bud Pentagon".

Old Fashioned, Old Friend, an Oldie, but a Goodie…
Wearing Hot Fudge as an "Ice Cream Hoodie".

Butterscotch & Pineapple, make their presence known…
Add some Raspberries, who are Cousins to the Scone.

Its Top Hat made, of Fluffy-Puffy, Whipped Cream…
Sprinkled, Chopped Walnuts, completes its theme.

Mustn't forget, Mustn't Leave Out…
Maraschino Cherries, a "Must Have". No Doubt.

A Walk on "The Wild Side", from Popsicle Sticks…
Here's to "The Banana Split", & its Chilly Tricks.

Written By: Charron M. Mollette (*09)

"FLOWER POWER"

Happiness is, Cheerful Daisies. Friendly. A Garden Gem...
Spreading Peace, with their Beauty, right down to the Stem.

Watercolor Violets, in their Purplish-Blue...
Showing Whimsical Etiquette, while playing "Peek-a-Boo".

Freshly Cut, Carnations, on a Pin-striped Gray Suit...
Tailored to Fit, Double-breasted to Boot.

Springtime's Drama Queen, is the Calla Lilly...
Is there anything more Perfect? That Question is Silly.

A Festival, in Celebration, of Tulip Bouquets & Bunches...
with Gentle Touches of Baby's Breath, for Casual Lunches.

The Backyard Delight. Rhododendrens in Bloom...
Then Beautifully Arranged, to Compliment any Room.

Windy Days, in the Month of May, with Playful Pushes…
Fuchsia Trees become Pals, with the Rose Bushes.

Always Proper & Polite, is the Punctual Primrose…
Sunflowers, are an Edible delight, as everyone knows.

Birds of Paradise, Flying Furiously, with Phenomenal Feats…
Iris is Petunia's, Old Neighbor, from "Sesame Street".

It's the Magic of Nature, that Weeds Love to Roam…
Like Dandelions, who are just, lookin' for a Good Home.

Written By: Charron M. Mollette (*09)

"The Butterfly"

A Little Bit of Everything,
and some things in between…
Is exactly why, a Butterfly, is Shy, and never mean.

Funtastic in Flight, with all of her might,
Fluttering her Wings…
Majestic & Meek, jamming a Blissful Beat,
doin' a "Zig-Zaggin" thing.

Playing Tag, with the Bees,
as she Frolics with ease, from Daisies to a Rose…
Showing Courage & Fame, A State Park in her Name?
Gossiping Ants, I Suppose.

The Spring Season Champ. Where does she like to Camp?
On Petunias, near my Window sill…
Her Wings can't be beat. Cool. Colorful. Neat.
even Dandelions, are given a Thrill.

Have you ever heard, the Soulful Mockingbird,
Dedicating to her, every Song?
"Good Morning!" "Good Day", then on her merry way,
It's a Treat, when she comes along.

Never thought, Never Knew
That when I was Blue,
a Smile, would soon Begin...
So, if you happen to see,
a Butterfly, on a Tree, Say "Hi"
you've just made a new Friend.

Written By: Charron M. Mollette (*09)

"Mink Slippers & Blue Jeans"

Softer than Cashmere, or a Cozy Afghan…
And even more Fun, than Ten "Disneyland's".

On the covers of "Vogue", Twisting Trendy..
Next to "Gucci", "Coach", & not to mention "Fendi".

Baggy, Super Saggy, these Threads are Contagious…
Bananas. Insane. Infectious. Outrageous.

Oxford Shirts, Pizza, & Missing Shoelaces…
Are simply no match, in small College Spaces.

The "Coolness" of "Sinatra", with the Hiss of a Snake…
Obeying the Speed Limit. A Visual Milkshake.

Cute as a Button, plus One Zillion Times Three...
Going from "Zero to Charming", Fast & Fancy.

Flavor. Five Pockets. Faded for Fun...
Like Cinderella's Glass Slipper, Envied by Everyone.

From a Runway in Paris, Urban Indigo-dipped...
Shades of Blueberries. Fully Loaded. Equipped.

Lethal, in their Language. An Anklet worn with Pride.
Groovy-Cool. Ol' School. Toe Rings, can't Hide...

Softer than Cashmere, or a Cozy Afghan...
And even more Fun, than Ten "Disneyland's".

Written By: Charron M. Mollette (*09)

"The Snow Queen"

Imported Popsicles, and other Crazy, Cool Treats…
She Avalanches, Jack Frost, as he Frowns in defeat.

Pigeon-toed Penguins, use Igloos for Storm-dodging…
She's "The Cold War", when She is Ski Lodging.

Karat-Cake Diamonds, Platinum, Precious Rocks…
Doin' an Icicle Tango, over her "Tiffany" Blue Box.

She has Tricks, up her Sleeve, & is about to Uncloak…
Her Siberian Huskies. They're the Truth. No Joke.

An Ice-berg gated Castle, with Protective Polar Bears…
At her North Pole Amusement Park, Whipping its Chilly Air.

Beneath, a Buttermilk Sky, Snow Flurries in Flight…
At a Sweltering Climate, Thirty-Two Fahrenheit.

Windshields, need Scraping, Studded Tires & Chains…
Twirling, Figure-Eights, from Icy, Frigid Rain.

A Powerful Punch, that begins to Snowball…
In the Month of January, a "Freeze Fest" for All.

Its the Yearly Arrival, from an "Ice Cube" Limousine…
The Numbing, Bittersweet, Wraith, of Winter's "Snow Queen".

Written By: Charron M. Mollette (*09)

"Purple"

Jimi Hendrix and His Guitar, made this Color, Hazy...
It's the Cool Shade, of a Song, Turning Prince, Umbrella Crazy.

It's the Soul, of author Alice Walker, with the Ribbons of Spring...
It's Meadows, Iris', & Lilac Trees, breathing Mood into Everything.

It's Crisp, Refreshing Soda, or Summer Plums that are Divine...
Blossoming Vineyards, around the World,
creating the Perfect Wine.

The "Winking" Amethyst Stone, & "Blinking" Tanzanite Gem...
It's the Color of Medal Hearts, for Soldiers, as we Honor them.

It's the Embracing, Swirling, Motion, as
the Sun fades from the Sky...
It's the Bashful, Beauty, of Lavender, on the Wings of a Dragonfly.

Written By: Charron M. Mollette (*07)

"NEW SUNDAY HAT"

From a Little Store Window, a Vision to Behold…
A Stylish Hat, that hadn't been Sold.

On a Street, sat a Hat, at a Corner Boutique…
Built from African Heritage, Surpassing Unique.

Classy, Triple Sassy, a Derby-Lover's Delight…
Eye Candy, Delicious, quite a Scrumptious Sight.

The Perfect Easter Bonnet, a Wooden Stand, for a Perch…
Silent Beauty, a Halo, as Mahalia Jackson in Church.

Cuteness, to Boot ness. More "Hip" than Motown…
A Designer Necessity, and Defining Crown.

A First Sunday must, this Twisted-made Hat…
Simple & Sweet, for Runway "Kats".

From Boring to Beautiful, to "Diva", to Queen"…
Sporting, The Finest Hat, the World has ever seen.

Like Sweet Potato Pie, Lullabies, or Honeycombs…
Hats are the Porch Light, showing that your Heart, is at Home.

For Goodness Sake. More Good & Bad News…
A New Hat is Nothing, without some "New Shoes".

From a Little Store Window, a Vision to Behold…
A Stylish Hat, that has just been Sold!

Written By: Charron M. Mollette (*09)

"THE BACK-PACK BLUES"

I Sleep Walk to the Bathroom, Brush my Face, Wash my Teeth…
Wishing I was still under my Blankets, &
Layers of Quilts underneath.

Feeling Khaki & Kinda' Preppy, I went from Gloomy to Glad…
Ironed a White Oxford Shirt, & a Hoodie of Green Plaid.

Scholastic & Savvy, while Curriculum Scared…
The Theory of Learning, helps me, be better Prepared.

Bulging Books, in my Backpack, weighing a Ton, if not more…
I was Studying until Dawn. Fell asleep on the Floor.

A Mad Dash to School, on a Bus Load of Fumes…
Mustn't be Late. Gotta Roll. Gotta Zoom.

Scholars & Professors, Scramble to their Classes…
with my Textbooks, Pens, Pencils, & "Study-Hall" Passes.

Instructors are Mentors, while remaining Students for Life…
Take Life Lessons in Spoonfuls, not a dull Butter Knife.

School isn't just a Building, with Doors to walk through…
It's Spiritual Teachings, where you learn about You.

Written By: Charron M. Mollette (*09)

"CHARMING"

She's the Guru of Gothic. Medieval with Grace...
A Home Décor, made of Leather, Blue Denim, & Lace.

She's a Fashion Icon, Top Designers adore her...
A Warm-Loving Cover Girl, who wears Gucci Faux Furs.

She Sings in the Rain, & Overcast Gloomy Days...
with it's Howling Winds, & Evil, Wicked, Ways.

Her Mercedes, has a Heart, filled with Sinister Tricks...
like Ravens into the Night, Faster than a Witch's Broomstick.

She's like the "Great Gatsby", hosting Formal Affairs...
A Trillion Dollar Business, Designing Sterling Flatware.

She's got Rhythm, like "Sinatra", as Fans follow her Flow...
She's Fearless, as Ichabod Crane, from Sleepy Hollow.

At the Stroke of Midnight, she got a Crazy Notion...
The Truth is, she invented, the Jekyll-Hyde Potion.

Living, deep in the Depths, of her very Soul...
Is the Spirit of Disneyland, so she'll never grow Old.

She's Royalty, A Vixen, a Zillion Times Three...
She's the Guru of Gothic, quite Charming, is She.

Written By: Charron M. Mollette (*09)

"Rims"

Black Denim Upholstery. Silver Chrome. Tight...
Sunny Afternoon, feelin' like Friday Night.

Weaving through Traffic, a Daily Task...
"Is that a New Bentley?", is what others ask.

A Concede Muffler, Better than Good...
Head Spinner, Show Winner, as we roll through "The Hood".

Sixty-Five Mustangs, or Sixty-Threes...
Have plenty of Trunk space, with Monogrammed Keys.

Limo-Tinted Windows, enhancing One's Vision...
Full Coverage Insurance, if in a Collision.

All-Weather Tires, Settling the Score...
Throttles & Hemi's, Horsepower & More.

A Hip, sort of "Hooptie", not a Tuna Can Scrub...
Funky-Fresh &Fantastic, are my Twenty-Inch "Dubs".

Written By: Charron M. Mollette (*09)

"BASKETBALL IS…"

Hi -Top, "Converse All-Stars", dressed in Chuck Taylor Blue…
Extra Large Shorts & Jersey, an Ol' School, Point of View.

Dribblin' Downtown, with Five Seconds to Shoot…
The Globe-Trotters are Funky, and make Handsome Loot.

Double-Team, Pick-N-Roll, or Personal Fouls…
A Pep Talk, from the Coach, to never throw in the Towel.

"Final Four" Ticket chances? It all depends…
On who has the best luck, may the Best Person Win.

The Legendary, Michael Jordan, is the "Houdini" of Hoops…
Explosive, are the "Hand Tricks", of Leslie & Swoopes.

Slam-Dunking, Trophies, filling Bookshelves…
Exercise True Sportsmanship, a Zillion times Twelve.

At Ruckers, in New York City, it's between "Shirts & Skins"…
Graffiti decorates the Background, of a Twirling Lay-Up-Backspin.

It's Wilson Leather, receiving the Encores, & Utmost Respect…
The Scoreboard is a Philosopher, One would Suspect.

Hi -Top, "Converse All-Stars", dressed in Chuck Taylor Blue…
Extra Large Shorts & Jersey, from an Ol' School, point of View.

Written By: Charron M. Mollette (*09)

"The Football Fan"

He's a Gridiron gladiator, the "Seahawks "12ᵗʰ Man…
A First Round Draft Pick. The Ultimate Fan.

At the Rose Bowl, Fiesta, Sugar, or Cotton…
He's an All American, who won't be forgotten.

A Locker full of Souvenirs, with his Helmet & Cleats…
A Jim Zorn signed Jersey, Growling at Defeat.

Who'll be the "NFL" Champs? It all depends…
It starts with Season Tickets, to see the Pig Skin.

From Coaching to Coin Toss, from "Bootleg" to Beer…
He's "Super Bowl" Commercials. He's why Cheerleaders Cheer.

His Knowledge of Clipping, could fill
Ten Thousand Bookshelves…
showing True Sportsmanship, a Zillion times Twelve.

"Gatorade" in his Veins. An Astroturf Architect…
He's a Scoreboard Philosopher, One would Suspect.

His Touchdown Dance, was on "ESPN"…
causing Stadium Frenzy, with his Twirling Backspin.

He's a Gridiron Gladiator, the "Seahawks "12ᵗʰ Man…
A First Round Draft Pick. The Ultimate Fan.

Written By: Charron M. Mollette (*09)

"The Checkered Flag"

Driven by Determination. It's how NASCAR came to be…
It's how an Ordinary Man, became the Legend "Number 3".

On the Oval Tracks, it's the Symbol of being Swift …
At the "Yakima Speedway", the Lead position can Shift.

The "Pit Crew" & Mechanics, Crank Out more Fuel…
Peeling Off, Spinning Out, are Unwritten Rules.

Part of "The Indy 500", or the Rally of Stock cars…
On Grass tracks, Vintage Vehicles, become "Super Stars".

The Daredevils of Daytona. Winston Cup. Formula One…
have their Endurance tested, under the "Swedish Midnight Sun".

Four on the Floor, Re-entry, or a "Cool" Chassis…
From Go-Karts, to Grid Starts, or a Hot Rod that's Classy.

Some "Straightaway" Battles, Spoil Slipstreaming…
Double Clutching for First, Winner's Circle Dreaming.

The "S - Bend", Tucking In, a Turn called a "Hairpin"…
Hit the Groove, being Smooth, & Ready to Win.

Driven by Determination. It's how HOT Wheels came to be…
It's how an Ordinary Man, became the Legend "Number 3".

Written By: Charron M. Mollette (*12)

"Easy Rider"

Legendary, as Mount Rushmore, or "The Sturgis Run"…
through the Black Hills of Dakota, greeting the Sun…

"Harley Davidson" Freedom, on the Wide open Road…
Old School "Bobber" & "Pitchfork", won't be Overshadowed.

Born to be Wild, on a "Blue Linx", with Ease…
Hugging the Highways. Kindness, comes in "Threes".

Perfect Precision, to Compliment Parking Spaces…
The "Little Red" Leader, has Stylish Graces.

Cooler than "Elvis", or Popcorn at the Drive-In…
Propelled by, an Internal Combustion Engine.

A Sight-Seeing, Time-Traveler, with Bionic Speed…
is the "Orange Knucklehead", a Nice Bike indeed.

"Black Widow" & "Dixie" Choppers, don't 'Shimmy' or 'Shake'…
Custom Wheels & Spokes, with the "Hiss" of a Snake.

A Moment of Silence. A Time to Reflect…
To Dare-Devil "Knievel", goes much Respect.

Legendary, as Mount Rushmore, or "The Sturgis Run"…
through the Black Hills of Dakota, greeting the Sun.

Written By: Charron M. Mollette (*08)

"Cookie Monster"

Last night, I invaded the Kitchen, searching for a Savory Treat …
Prisoner, to a Haunting Craving…
of Chocolate Chip Cookies, so Sweet.

Sliding on my Slippers, after springing out of Bed…
the Chocolate Chips, and Pecans…
were hiding behind the Bread.

Born from a Family Recipe, not long in the Jar, will it stay…
This Rare Goodie Mixture, will Tickle the Palate…
Exquisite in Every way.

After a Hug, from the Oven, not One crumb, will be shared…
A brief moment to Cool, then Gobbled 'em up…
These Cookies could not be compared.

Chocolate Chip Cookies. The Best Invention,
A Dessert with High Acclaim…
A Gift, from the Cupboard. A Wonderful thing.
"Perfection", should Retire its Name.

Written By: Charron M. Mollette (*09)

"CATFISH & CORNBREAD"

When I was Young, I helped Granny,
in the Kitchen, we'd be...
Boiling Mustard and Collard Greens,
While the "Soaps", were on T.V.

Fresh Catfish, from the Market,
Cornmeal, Pepper and Seasoning Salt...
It's "Aretha Franklin" Good,
and should, be kept in a Vault.

In every room, would be the Wonderful scent,
of Catfish, Ox Tails, or Neck Bones...
Counting my Blessings, before each Meal,
Prayers Precious, as Diamond Stones.

At Night, I'd Thank the Heavens,
before resting my Sleepy Head…
For the Gifts of Faith and Family,
Granny's Catfish and Cornbread.

Feeding the Soul, like a Fairytale,
Like a Castle, with a Drawbridge…
Capturing the Hearts of Many,
as a Late night Snack, from the Fridge.

When I was Young, I helped Granny,
in the Kitchen, we'd be…
Boiling Mustard and Collard Greens,
While the "Soaps", were on T.V.

Written By: Charron M. Mollette (*08)

"THE PAINTER"

A Painting Princess, with a Passion. Whose Creations Beautify...
Her Priceless Works of Art, are Whispers of the Sky.

This Gifted One, puts her Heart, into every Brush stroke...
Giving a Forest, Movement. Bringing to Life, The Mighty Oak.

Her Smile should be Framed, Cuter than Toy Trains & Wagons...
Her Beauty is the Reason, that Knights have Slayed Dragons.

A Storyteller on Canvas, as a Writer's every Page...
But Smoother than Ballerinas, Twirling across the Stage.

She's "Da Vinci, Picasso, & Georgia O'Keeffe"...
Expressing the Dance, of Autumn's Falling Leaf.

Artistic, Simplistic, with Style & with Grace...
She's the "Poet of Portraits", without having to Trace.

Watercolors are Sunsets. She captures its Blush…
The Moon's Charm is Revealed, in her Gallery of Airbrush.

The Fashion House of "Valentino", is embraced by Italy…
Yet, No One has Mastered a Mural, better than She.

Finger painting, is Expression, not just a Name…
This Graffiti is for a Sweetie, and painting is her Game.

A Painting Princess, with a Passion. Whose Creations Beautify…
Her Priceless Works of Art, are Whispers of the Sky.

Written By; Charron M. Mollette (*09)

"The Photographer"

He's the Knight of "Nikon" Cameras. The "Kat of "Canon Cool"…
'Made' from "Minolta's Mafia", & "Polaroid's" Old School.

In Motion Pictures the Silver Screen, serves as the Perfect Frame…
He's skilled in "Fuji" Film, as Quick as Dragon Flames.

"Click, Click", no Trick, like the Legendary "Gordon Parks"…
Snapshots worth a Thousand Words, developed in the Dark.

Talented, gracing the cover of "Time", & the World of Fashion…
Dramatic as a Photo Finish, from "Kentucky Derby" Passion.

An Ambassador of "Ambrotype", an early Glass Negative…
That's backed by a Dark surface, that appears quite Positive.

Like "McCartney's" Lens, his Images, are Photo Thrills …
From "The San Francisco Bridge", to other Black & White Stills.

A "Kodak" King, doing his Thing, unlike
"Paparazzi" or Media Press…
Sharp as a Knife, capturing Wildlife, creating Happiness.

'Wertheimer' Portraits are Illustrations, of "Elvis" frozen in Time…
Creating Visual Keepsakes, is the Close-up of this Rhyme.

He's a "Photog", staying focused. He's an Artist. A Shutterbug…
He's "Super Fly", not Camera Shy, creating Visual "Hugs".

He's the Knight of "Nikon" Cameras. The "Kat of "Canon Cool"…
'Made' from "Minolta's Mafia", & "Polaroid's" Old School.

Written By: Charron M. Mollette (*08)

"The Deer Hunter"

He's the Deer Hunter. His Game is Sporting Goods…
Searching for Elk, in the Misty Mountains, of the Woods.

"Patience" is the Prey. His Eagle Eyes are on the Loose…
True Marksmanship, for Wild Turkey or Goose.

In Camouflage for his Country. Patriotic & Calm…
A Son. A Freedom Biker, through the Pages of Viet Nam.

Half Man. Half Time Traveler, back One Hundred Years…
Seen by fellow Hunters, but Invisible to Deer.

Dramatic as "DeNiro's Character", played on the Silver Screen…
with a Little "Elmer Fudd", sprinkled in between.

A Gentleman, Spirited with "The Fox & Hounds"…
Believes in Forest Beauty, & how Loud it's Silence sounds.

Legend has it, before Dawn, he Wrestles Grizzly Bears…
A Rifleman in Pursuit, geared with Campfire Silverware.

Part of a "Dynamic Duo", telling "Ducky Tales" about Quails…
'Tis the Season, for his Quest, of the Canadian Trails.

He's the Deer Hunter. His Game is Sporting Goods…
Searching for Elk, in the Misty Mountains, of the Woods.

Written By: Charron M. Mollette (*07)

"The Duck Hunter"

"Patience" is the Prey. The "Muscovy" are on the Loose…
Testing True Marksmanship, for "Crested" Duck or Goose.

There's a Sportsman who knows, when it's Diving Duck Season…
"White Pekin" or "Aylesbury", are just some of the Reasons.

In Camouflage, for "Khaki Campbell", near a Hunting Lodge…
The "Indian Runner" Ducks, trying to cleverly Dodge.

Half Man. Half Time Traveler, back One Hundred Years…
Seen by fellow Hunters, but Invisible to Fear.

He's that Thrilling Action Hero, played on the Silver Screen…
with a Little "Elmer Fudd", sprinkled in between.

Always in pursuit, where "Canvasbacks" are found…
He listens for the "Whistling", & how Loud its Silence sounds.

Legend has it, before Dawn, he Wrestles Grizzly Bears…
so he can be a better Rifleman, geared in Outerwear.

He's part of a "Dynamic Duo", telling "Tales" about Quails…
'Tis the Season, for his Quest, of the Canadian Trails.

More famous than "Donald" or "Daffy". in the "Perching" Game…
He Dabbles in Duck Hunting, remember his name.

Written By: Charron M. Mollette (*08)

"MR. & MRS."

Faithfully, on their Journey, as each other's "Keepsake"…
Engagement. The Vows. The First Dance & Wedding Cake.

"Bonnie & Clyde". 2-gether. 4-Ever…
They're the Words & Music, of "Stormy Weather".

They're Island Castaways, making Castles on the Beach…
The Moon may be Too far to grasp, but it's Not beyond their reach.

They're Comfort &Joy, like Winter Hats & Mittens…
with the Charm & Innocence, as a Calendar of Kittens.

They have Magic, like a Picnic, on a Sunny Day…
They're Stars in the Galaxy, plus the Milky Way.

They're Time Travelers, taking the Ultimate Trip…
More Fun than a Banana Split, topped with Chocolate Chips.

Always with Kind Words to say. Teenagers holding Hands…
A King & his Queen, from a Fairytale Land.

Twenty-Four Karat, Solid Gold, Memories for a Locket…
Their Love Deeper, than the Ocean or Designer Denim pockets.

They're "Paper & Pen", A Love Story, with
things Borrowed & Blue…
Living the words of Scripture. Testaments Old & New.

Written By: Charron M. Mollette (*09)

"Anything"

Adapt to Ad-libs, by Avoiding Awkward Angles...
Like Adjectives And Adverbs, And other "Verbal Triangles".

Always Awesome is Autumn, with Auburn-colored Afternoons...
So are April And August, And eating Apricots with a spoon.

Amid Acorn trees, picnic Ants Anticipate...
The Arrival of Applesauce, Alongside Angel-food Cake.

In Addition to Algebra, or Anthropology Class...
Acute Accounting is Analyzed, in order to pass.

At the Academy Awards, Actors Appreciate Applause...
Giving Admiring fans Autographs, just because.

Adventurous Adidas, Appealing Apparel for feet...
Athens, Greece, the Olympics where Athletes compete.

Automobiles get Angry, with Abnormal Attitudes...
If traveling Across America, without gasoline for food.

Asteroids are Acrobats, while Androids Are not...
Aerospace And Astronomy, for brave Astronauts.

Attractive, Ageless Antiques, Acquire Attention...
And, Acknowledge Advice, whenever it's mentioned.

Written By: Charron M. Mollette (*07)

"DEMOLITION MAN"

His Kingdom, is a Courtyard, of Destructive Devotion...
His Ultimate Goal, is to be the Last One in Motion.

He's Frowned "Ford" fenders. His Mission, to Obliterate...
Crashing then Dashing, towards a "Chevy" to Eliminate.

In this Super bowl Smash-up, he will Erase...
Foes trying to De-throne him, but Fail to Deface.

He has nothing to Hide. He has Nothing to Prove...
Always Ten Steps ahead. Always on the Move.

The Master of Mufflers, dueling a Muddy War...
A Legend who Believes, that's what Rear Bumpers are for.

Rapid Fire, from his Tires. Deleting. Destroying.
Treating Trucks like Tuna Cans, kinda' like "Tonka" Toying.

Does he Crumple & Crinkle? Will this Duke Demolish?
Fun follows his Flow, like the "Shine" from Shoe Polish.

Without a Doubt, bragging rights are the Prize…
The Cowboys of Cars, use Vehicles to Vaporize.

In Seconds, he's Here, then he's There, then he's Gone…
He's "Demolition Man", & his Name is "Jon".

His Kingdom, is a Courtyard, of Destructive Devotion…
His Ultimate Goal, is to be the Last One in Motion.

Written By: Charron M. Mollette (*08)

"The Everything Burger"

What's the Number One Attraction? What takes center stage?
It's the perfect Sandwich, it's recipe, in a vaulted cage.

The work of a sheer Genius, is this edible piece of Art...
A handed down tradition, right from the very start.

At the Playground, for the hungry, cravings are put to shame...
There's a certain Burger Bistro, where Hospitality is the Game.

Every taste bud is tested, with a tempting aroma...
From the "School of Flipology", with a Master's Diploma.

A Culinary Mad Scientist, unveils tasty experiments...
A Feast fit for Royalty, along with every Lady and Gent.

Simply Delicious is the Menu, and it's no surprise...
It defines the word "Smooth", like ketchup on cheddar fries.

Lettuce, Hot links, and tomatoes, giving groupie Love…
Custom engineered, perfect like Hand and Glove.

Pickles do their "Pimpin", crowning this Prince of Patties…
You'll want to slap yourself, and your Great Granddaddy.

Flashing Paparazzi, frenzy fans, and also friends…
Adore the treat of a Lifetime, it's unlike other Burger trends.

Icy Waterfalls of Soda, quenching any thirst…
Before a DMV line starts to form, it's wise to be there first.

It's got the Heart of Joe Louis, with it's Knock-out Punch…
It's "The Everything Burger", the cure, the answer to lunch.

Written By: Charron M. Mollette (*08)

"PINK"

Precious, Perfection, are Diamonds,
Along with the Joy, that they bring…
It's Cotton Candy & Balloons at the Circus,
or Bouquets of Carnations, that Sing.

It's the Mood, of a Candle-light Dinner Party,
Poached Salmon & Champagne, with Friends…
It's the Label, of a Gin & Bitters, British Cocktail,
Leaving most "Three Sheets to the Wind".

It's the Happiness, in a Sno-Cone,
or a Busy, Lemonade Stand…
It's the Fifth or smallest Finger,
The most unique of all, on the Hand.

It's the Cool Theme, of a certain Cartoon,
written by Henry Mancini…
It's Silly & Tickles like Bubble Gum,
Funny as "Dumbo" in a Bikini.

Brightly Clever, always Honest,
with its innocent Wink…
When defining Pretty Things,
Trust in the Shyness of Pink.

Written By: Charron M. Mollette (*09)

"Black"

Shiny Onyx Cuff Links, for a Tuxedo Affair…
A "Black Belt" in "Judo", against a "Karate" Dare.

"The Temptations" & "The Four Tops" defining "Rock & Roll"…
Ivory-Black Piano Keys, created "Motown's" Soul.

It's Delicious Bean Soup, Ground Pepper, or Peas…
It's a Pot of Coffee, so waking up is a Breeze.

Lost in Pitch Blackness, of Count Dracula's Cape…
From the "Mark of Zorro", There is no Escape.

Through the South Dakota Hills, Black Stallions run Free…
while Ravens, spread their Wings, over the "Black Sea".

The Card Game of "Black Jack", called "Twenty One"…
Exciting "Roulette" & "Checkers", which can also be Fun.

Rich as "Forest Cake" or the Delicious "Pearl"…
A Black Hole in the Universe, or the Deep Underworld.

A Black Diamonds Brilliance, Sweeter than Blackberry Pie…
Spinning Tales of Black Magic, Circling the Night Sky.

Mysterious, in its Silence, amid its Powerful Force…
What is the Opposite of White? Why it's Black of course.

Written By: Charron M. Mollette (*09)

"White"

"White" is the Essence of Everything...
Like Sparkling "Diamonds", in a Platinum Ring.

"Pearls", Twirls, & Curls, for a Blushing Bride...
Clean, "White-wall Tires", on a Convertible Ride.

It's at the "White House", where the President dwells...
Mailing "Envelopes", are replaced by E-mails.

Fluffy, Soft "Cotton", billowy "Clouds"...
"Snow-covered Mountains", standing Proud.

"Whipped Cream, Alabaster, or Ivory" Silk...
For Strong Healthy Bones, drink plenty of "Milk".

A "French Manicure", is truly "The Most"...
And we all know "Casper, the Friendly Ghost".

Double checking your List, for the Supermarket…
Bags of "Rice, Flour, & Sugar", you mustn't forget.

"Wall Street's" White Collar, is "Financially Cool"…
The "Cue Ball" Maestros, the Game of Pool.

The Classic Ballet, Tchaikovsky's "Swan Lake"…
"Liquid Paper" is used, for Writting mistakes.

"Lilies & Daisies", are the Signs of Spring…
"White" is the Essence of Everything.

Written By: Charron M. Mollette (*08)

"Blue"

The Color of Half-broken Crayons,
The Owner, a Proud Six Year Old…
The Mood of Cool Jazz, or a Painted Truck,
Like Family, to never be Sold.

The Glow of berries, picked for a Pie,
First Prize Ribbons, at the State Fair…
It's the Suede Shoe, sung by "The King"
Who also sang "Teddy Bear".

That catchy Song written about the round Moon,
Wolves Howl, at its Sight…
The Topaz Jewels, or a Warm Woven Quilt,
Keeping you company at Night.

The Shade of Worn Jeans, with Holey Knees,
You Don't dare throw away, or replace…
The Properties on the "Monopoly" Board,
The Classic "Boardwalk" & "Park Place".

It's the Laughter, or the part of the Rainbow,
That holds an Incredible, Hue…
It's Nature's Best work by far,
& it's the Color of "Blue".

Written By: Charron M. Mollette (*09)

"RED"

Fire Engines, Chili Peppers, rare Steak, & Wine...
A Penny for Roses, from Cupid is Fine.

Stop Signs, prevent Danger, Be careful Beware...
Fans Laughed & Loved Lucy, with her Strawberry Hair.

"Rocky" & the Velvet Rope, dueling in Round Eight...
Delicious Apples, Home-grown, from Washington State.

On The Red Carpet, for Academy Night...
The shy Planet of Mars, glowing Cinnamon Light.

Candy Cane Stripes, the spinning Roulette Wheel...
"The Cincinnati Reds" & "Red Sox", give Baseball Appeal.

A "Chevy Corvette", with Suede Interior...
Cherry Checkers, Duel Black, to be reigned Superior.

A Lady Bug's Luck, flies as a Kite...
Flying First Class, for a Late Red Eye Flight.

"Coca Cola Classic", Cold refreshing, & Clean...
Dorothy's Slippers, took her Home, on the Silver Screen.

Kaleidoscopes & Rainbows, Twirl in my Head...
The Boldest of all, is the Color of "Red".

Written By: Charron M. Mollette (*09)

"GREEN"

It's the Color of Jade, or the Emerald Jewel…
It's that "Dr. Seuss Story", that was read in School.

In the City of "Oz", a Lost Girl, met a "Wiz"…
A Big Shot, who specialized in the "Wish-Granting" Biz.

It's "Kermit the Frog". "The Tortoise & the Hare"…
Stashed away Currency, for Zillionaires.

"Mother Nature" Maestros, a "Cucumber Salad"…
Mint Chocolate Chip Ice Cream. A "Shamrock" Shake Ballad.

It's Bluegrass from Kentucky, it's Music. It's Spring…
It's Grasshoppers & Lily Pads. It's Everything.

Spinach not Broccoli, gave "Popeye" his Punch…
"The Incredible Hulk", clobbered Villains before Lunch.

The swaying of Palm Trees, off of Waikiki…
Part of a Traffic Light, the Third Color of Three.

It's the Shade of the Mighty, & Elite "Green Beret"…
Or a Joyous Celebration, called "Saint Patrick's Day".

It's a Way of Life, taking Care of Mother Earth…
Recycling, giving back, for our Planet's Rebirth.

It's the Color of Jade, or the Emerald Jewel…
It's that "Dr. Seuss Story", that was read in School.

Written By: Charron M. Mollette (*09)

"Casino"

Luck is a Lady, She's Stacks of Poker Chips...
She's the Heartbeat of Las Vegas, & the "Glitz" of the Strip.

At Scenic Lake Tahoe or Downtown Reno...
Players & Patrons, try their "Skillz" at Keno.

Action-packed "Caesar's Palace", whether Right or Wrong...
"Temptation" is Singing, "The Gambler" Song.

Along Atlantic City's Boardwalk, a Romantic sight...
A New Heavyweight Champion, wins a Sold-out Prize Fight.

Monte Carlo, feels like winning the Lottery, Twice...
Hoping for Seven, not "Snake Eyes", with the Roll of the Dice.

"The One Armed Bandit", Notorious on the Scene...
Go from Nickels, to Shiny Silver Dollar Machines.

Excitement grows, with each Roulette Wheel Spin…
Red or Black Double Zero, Odd or Even.

The Card Game "Blackjack", also called "Twenty-One"…
Trying to Bluff with Two Pair, is sometimes Fun.

Frank, Dean & Sammy, "The Rat Pack" & Live Bands…
Performed at "The Flamingo", & also "The Sands".

Luck is a Lady, She's Stacks of Poker Chips…
She's the Heartbeat of Las Vegas, & the "Glitz" of the Strip.

Written By: Charron M. Mollette (*08)

"THE DESIGNER"

His Creations, more Famous, than Vera Wang Gowns…
Worn by "Miss Universe", outshining her Crown.

An Elegant Collection, what Runways are for…
As 'Fabulous' as Chanel, or the House of Dior.

He's Sophisticated Style. He's Gucci Handbags…
Just as Oscar De la Renta's, Signature name tag.

When "Starlets" Step out, for the Paparazzi, & Press…
It's his Designs, overshadowing, Valentino's Red Dress.

Yves Saint Laurent, may heat Winter & Fall…
But this Amazing Magician, defines Masquerade Ball.

Ferocious as Ferragamo, spanning the Globe…
with Jaw-dropping Trends, for "Spring-Summer" Wardrobes.

He Rocks "Glamazons", He's "Far Out" like "The Doors"…
He's more Gifted than Ralph Lauren, or Michael Kors.

Jet-Setters, Wall-Streeters, need to catch a Clue…
He's Edgy, like Heatherette, & compliments Jimmy Choo.

Edith Head, dressed Hollywood, mastering the Game…
but there's a New Kid in town, a Designer with infamous fame.

Written By: Charron M. Mollette (*08)

"Mr. and Mrs."

They're Today and Tomorrow, with a little Now and Then…
representing all Love Stories, written in Pen.

Together. Forever. Without Left there's no Right…
Like a Book needs its Pages, or a Day needs Sunlight.

They have the strength of Railroad Tracks, curvy in Design…
Taking a Sentimental Journey, where Memories are defined.

His & Hers. Lock & Key. All of The Above…
Like Fred & Wilma Flintstone. Like Teenagers in Love.

Add, Subtract, Multiply, then Divide…
They're the Perfect Equation, a Groom & his Bride.

They're Lyrics & Music, with the Brilliance of a Gem…
The "Two Dollar Bill", was named after them.

Half This & Half That, where Two become One…
Where Love is Everlasting, where the Moon meets the Sun.

Jumping the Broom, as their Hearts Zoom, the Old Fashion way…
Old & New, Borrowed & Blue, with each passing Day.

They're Today and Tomorrow, with a little Now and Then…
representing all Love Stories, written in Pen.

Written By: Charron M. Mollette (*08)

"THE D.J."

He's Adidas. He's "Kangol's". He's solid Gold chains…
Hip Hop's melody, a must see, 'cause he Reigns.

The Duke of all DJ's, stand back fifty feet…
as he scratches the cuts, never missing a Beat.

Allergic to "Haters", they make him sneeze…
He's cooler than winter, 'causing Jack Frost to freeze.

Don't blink, or you'll miss him. Talented. Unique…
Paparazzi swarm and hover, around this freestyle freak.

A Legend. An Icon, gracing every front page…
Turntable gifted, wanted center stage.

Break dancers, Pop lockers, all flock to the spot…
Giving Love and Respect, to the "Houdini of Hot".

He gobbles up rhythm and spins out of spite…
You'll be lost in the Matrix, against this Jedi knight.

Don't worry, be happy, your feet will thank you…
His net worth, since birth? One trillion times two.

A Grandmaster with flash, Ol' School with flare…
His Vinyl vocabulary, stopping suckers who stare.

He's Adidas. He's "Kangol's". He's solid Gold chains…
He's The "DJ", a must see, 'cause he Reigns.

Written By: Charron M. Mollette (*16)

"Drum Sticks"

"Rolling Stone" magazine, has him on the Front page...
Screaming Fans, utter Chaos, when he takes the stage.

Groupies hide in his dressing room, fulfilling their crush...
He and "Neil Pert", shared a Tour Bus with "Rush".

He's "Sick" on the Symbols. He Rocks the Kick Drum...
"U 2" are Spellbound, by his Rattle and Hum.

The "Ramones", a garage band, their Music, Insane...
A Duet, unplugged, with the Legend "Cobain".

An Alaskan Frontiersman, venture if you dare...
He's nimble, with a Thimble, the curious stop and stare.

Showcasing his Gift, Skyrocketing to Fame...
Becoming the Boom, one and all know his name.

In Europe, with "Kiss". A Las Vegas kind of "Kat"...
A "Ringo" sort of Lingo, as he tips his High Hat.

Magical with his Drumsticks, twirling with jive...
He's the Essence of "Woodstock" in Extreme Overdrive.

Written By: Charron M. Mollette (*14)

"STRINGS"

At the age of Nine, a romance began…
between a Girl, a Cello, and her gifted hands.

The Chamber of Music was lost, but she Found it…
A Julliard prodigy, her Spirit surrounds it.

"Kramer vs. Kramer". Best Picture in Seventy-nine…
String instruments storytelling, playing softly behind.

The Double Bass, is full of Grace, in size and pitch…
If Bravery were money, then she was born rich.

She's the Violin, they could be Twins, having poetic tone…
Strong and mellow, on the Cello, a soulful "Saks-o-phone".

Music married Medicine. A Vivaldi symphony…
Two Family Trees, among Honeybees, in perfect Harmony.

She's Radio City. Sold out Carnegie Hall…
The New Year's Eve darling, as Times Square drops the ball.

Overture. Curtain. Lights, in prayer for Seven days…
a Cellist we'll remember, as she forever plays.

Written By: Charron M. Mollette (*13)

"FRIENDSHIP"

You're "Lucy", I'm "Ethel", when two worlds Collide…
Butch & Sundance, would have nowhere to hide.

We're Today & Tomorrow, with a little Now & Then…
Representing every Novel, written in Pen.

Like "Martin & Lewis", we do our own Stunts…
You're that Fairy Godmother, I read as a child once.

Well-matched, an Odd Couple. We're "Wilma & Betty"…
And a Bond, twice as Strong, as Meatballs & Spaghetti.

Together, we're Clever, without Left there's no Right..
You're the Book, I'm the Words, You are my Sunlight.

The Two-Dollar Bill, was named after us…
We often get the Giggles, like kids on a School Bus.

Add, Subtract, Multiply, then Divide…
Summed Up, our Friendship is Grand Canyon wide.

We "Hello" & "Hi", with you I have Fun…
Our journey, together has just begun.

Written by: Charron M. Mollette (*11)

"Hat Trick"

He's a Hot Shot. A Trickster, His "Bling" cold as Ice...
He's swift, as a 'Hat Trick", it'll make you blink twice.

A Face-off against Gretzsky, as he foolishly challenged him...
He got hammered on the glass, a Cross-
check made his pride look grim.

Like Olympic Gold, he's shimmers with Delight...
As a Star in the Cosmos, as a Hockey puck takes flight.

He's got a "Mighty Duck" soul. A Ranger. A Red Wing...
With the spirit of Canada, and a "Stanley Cup" ring.

Figure skaters, see you later, as he Twists and Twirls...
No cheater, he's neater, than a Peppermint swirl.

The Goal is quite simple. The point? Simply this...
His Two-One-Two Tactics, are Power Play bliss.

He's smooth as a Zamboni, as it glides on the rink...
If his laugh was a color, it would be tickled Pink.

Many have been placed, in the Penalty Box...
Failing to admit, that he truly rocks.

He's a Hot Shot. A Trickster, His "Bling" cold as Ice...
He's swift, as a 'Hat Trick", it'll make you blink twice.

Written By; Charron M. Mollette (*16)

"THE POSTCARD"

Dreaming I escape from my pillowcase...
To the picturesque homeland, of a friends birthplace.

The Quaint farming cottages, or "Dachas" by name...
Meeting famed Soccer Stars, of the popular game.

"Varenyky" or dumplings, dance over my head...
With a Hot bowl of "Borsch" with Butter and Bread.

Tip-toeing through flowers, with some in my hair...
A "Bandura" stringed instrument, in "Kharkiv Square".

"Shevchenko" and "Levytsky" give paintings lessons to me...
Their best work are the murals in "Kyiv", near the Black Sea.

Like a Friendly postcard, with a stamp upside down...
This country's beauty, would cure any frown.

Tradition and landscape, compliment the terrain...
Adding simplistic design, to the marvel of "Ukraine"

Written By: Charron M. Mollette (*03)

"Sushi Bar"

Far East of eating, unlike Fast Food Cafes…
Over-crowded canteens, a confusing maze.

A Show-Busy Bistro, for loved ones and friends…
Marinated in skills, profits of "Cheddar" or dividends.

A Cabaret of Cuisine, and Iron Chef Tricks…
Soothing Green Tea, a fresh set of Chopsticks.

From plate to palate, a feathery-light Spinach salad…
Skinny-dipping in Soy sauce, a delectable ballad.

Bulldozing taste buds, amid dining glamour…
Tangled up Bliss, and speechless grammar.

Samurai Spicy, switching Off to On…
Vegetarian suave. Your appetite? Gone.

Traffic-jammed with juicy, succulent "Sushi"…
More Live than Saturday Night, with John Belushi.

Written By: Charron M. Mollette (*16)

"BALL OF YARN"

When I grow up,
I want to be a Warm Sweater,
Staying soft, when I'm Shabby and Old.

Or even a scarf with Mittens to match,
To help battle the bitter cold.

I've romanced the notion,
I'm a Thick pair of socks,
Your feet, I will gladly rescue.

With age, a hole may sprout in the toe,
But I'll still be as good as new.

Wishful thinking, I suppose,
That someday I'll be a Ski Hat…
But for now, I'm just a Ball of Yarn,
A cheap toy, for this silly cat.

Written By: Charron M. Mollette (*16)

"Court Jester"

He's the Greatest Storyteller, of Tales to be told…
Tickling the Funny Bone, of both Young and Old.

Higher Jinx than Jerry Lewis. More Classy than "Carson"…
He's like "Richard Pryor" committing Ad-Lib arson.

With microphone in hand, in a Ginger "Snap"…
He'll have you in stitches, his punch lines are on tap.

A Smirk and a Smile, with Giggles and Grins…
He's the Quarterback of humor, where everyone wins.

Plenty of Heart, plenty of Laughter…
He's the Hurricane of Hilarious. He's Before and After.

Luck may be a Lady, but he is quite charming…
A Philosopher of Truth, his Wit is alarming.

A Comedy Club tour, has sold-out shows...
Paparazzi follow him, wherever he goes.

In Ten thousand seconds, before you can think...
The pride of all "Haters", are washed down the sink.

He's the Heavyweight Champ, of serious Chuckles...
He'll knock-out "Blue Mondays", with his verbal brass knuckles.

He's the Greatest Storyteller, of Tales to be told...
Tickling the Funny Bone, of both Young and Old.

Written By: Charron m. Mollette (*16)

48963188R00054

Made in the USA
San Bernardino, CA
09 May 2017